American Public Support for U.S. Military Operations from Mogadishu to Baghdad

Technical Appendixes

Eric V. Larson, Bogdan Savych

Prepared for the Arroyo Center

ARROYO CENTER

The research described in this report was sponsored by the United States Army under Contract No. DASW01-01-C-0003.

ISBN: 0-8330-3683-1

The RAND Corporation is a nonprofit research organization providing objective analysis and effective solutions that address the challenges facing the public and private sectors around the world. RAND's publications do not necessarily reflect the opinions of its research clients and sponsors.

RAND® is a registered trademark.

Published 2005 by the RAND Corporation
1776 Main Street, P.O. Box 2138, Santa Monica, CA 90407-2138
1200 South Hayes Street, Arlington, VA 22202-5050
201 North Craig Street, Suite 202, Pittsburgh, PA 15213-1516
RAND URL: http://www.rand.org/
To order RAND documents or to obtain additional information, contact
Distribution Services: Telephone: (310) 451-7002;
Fax: (310) 451-6915; Email: order@rand.org

Preface

This document contains the technical appendixes for a study that describes American public opinion toward the use of military force in support of the global war on terrorism (GWOT), delineates the sources of support and opposition, and identifies potential fault lines in support. The main document is Eric V. Larson and Bogdan Savych, *American Public Support for U.S. Military Operations from Mogadishu to Baghdad,* Santa Monica, CA: RAND Corporation, MG-231-A, 2004.

These appendixes describe bivariate and multivariate statistical analyses of respondent-level public opinion data from polling during the final stages of the U.S. military intervention in Somalia, the peace operations in Haiti, Bosnia, and Kosovo, the war against the Taliban and Al Qaeda in Afghanistan, and the overthrow of Saddam Hussein's Baathist regime in Iraq.

This research was sponsored by Chief, National Security Policy Division, Office of the Deputy Chief of Staff, G-3, Department of the Army. It was conducted in RAND Arroyo Center's Strategy, Doctrine and Resources Program. RAND Arroyo Center, part of the RAND Corporation, is a federally funded research and development center sponsored by the Army.

For more information on RAND Arroyo Center, contact the Director of Operations (telephone 310-393-0411, ex. 6419; FAX 310-451-6952; e-mail Marcy_Agmon@rand.org), or visit Arroyo's web site at http://www.rand.org/ard/.

Contents

Tables

CHAPTER ONE

Introduction

This set of technical appendixes provides illustrative results from our bivariate and multivariate statistical analyses of respondent-level datasets from polls conducted during the U.S. interventions in Somalia, Haiti, Bosnia, Kosovo, Afghanistan, and Iraq.

The results reported here are results from what we considered to be the "best" of the datasets for each case, not in the sense that the dataset yielded the best predictions, but in the sense that the question wordings that were used most closely approximated the conceptual meanings we had in mind for our independent variables (beliefs about the importance of the stakes, prospects for success, and likely costs, and party and information consumption) and dependent variables (support or, for Somalia, preference for withdrawal or escalation); we performed very many more statistical tests than those reported here, and these analyses yielded similar results.

This document is organized as follows:

- Appendix A provides the results of bivariate and multivariate statistical analyses of withdrawal and escalation sentiment on Somalia.
- Appendix B provides the results of our analyses of Haiti.
- Appendix C provides the results of our analyses of Bosnia.
- Appendix D provides results for Kosovo.
- Appendix E provides results for Afghanistan.
- Appendix F provides results for Iraq.

Statistical Results for Somalia

We used a family of statistical techniques called probit regression for our statistical modeling of individual-level preferences for withdrawal or escalation.

Withdrawal Sentiment

We first model respondents' preferences regarding staying in or withdrawing from Somalia, based upon data from an ABC News poll conducted on October 5, 1993, two days before the president's October 7 speech, and at a time when most national political leaders supported withdrawal.

Table A.1 provides the wording of the questions used to estimate our model.

Table A.1
Wording of Question in ABC News Somalia Poll, October 5, 1993

Variable	Question Wording
Withdrawal	Q3. Do you think the United States should keep troops in Somalia until there's a functioning civil government there that can run things, or do you think the U.S. should pull its troops out of Somalia very soon, even if there is no functioning civil government in place?
Stakes	Q6. Do you think America's vital interests are at stake in Somalia or not?
Prospects	Q10. Just your best guess: Do you think the United States is going to get bogged down in a drawn-out military involvement in Somalia, or do you think the U.S. military involvement there will end quickly?

Table A.2 predicts preferences for withdrawing from or staying in Somalia; our hypothesis is that a belief in vital interests and good prospects for success would be associated with a willingness to stay, and the absence of that belief would be associated with a preference for withdrawal. The coefficients reflect the average (mean) change in probability of the dependent variable for an infinitely small change in the independent variable, or, in case of dummy variables, for a change from 0 to 1.

As shown, the model correctly predicts 63 percent of the respondents, and also shows that, as predicted, a willingness to stay hinged on the belief that the United States had vital interests involved, and good prospects for a successful outcome, whereas a preference for withdrawal was associated with a failure to see vital interests or good prospects in Somalia. Unfortunately, fewer than one in three actually believed that the United States had vital interests in Somalia, and a plurality of 47 percent thought the United States was going to get bogged down in Somalia (by comparison, only 44 percent thought U.S. involvement would end quickly), so the net result was lukewarm support for staying.

Table A.2
Marginal Probability from Probit Estimates of Withdrawal (Q3)

Variables	Change in Probability at Mean Values
Vital interests (q6)[†]	0.229 (0.063)***
Prospects (q10)[†]	0.167 (0.047)***
Party 1 if Republican[†]	0.023 (0.060)
Party 1 if Independent[†]	−0.056 (0.060)
Gender 1 if female[†]	−0.169 (0.048)***
Wald Chi-square (Prod > Chi2)	40.69 (0.000)
Log-likelihood	−227.656
Observations	401
Correctly specified	63%

SOURCE: ABC News, October 5, 1993. The withdrawal question was coded as 0 if the respondent wanted to pull out, and 1 if they wanted to keep troops in Somalia.
[†] dF/dx is for discrete change of dummy variable from 0 to 1.
* Significant at 10%.
** Significant at 5%.
*** Significant at 1%.
Robust standard error in parentheses.

Escalation Sentiment

Our modeling of escalation sentiment also confirmed the predicted relationship between escalation and beliefs about the stakes and prospects for success, which lends additional support to the correctness of the underlying model. Table A.3 provides the question wording for the variables we used to estimate the model.

In this dataset we had several questions that we were able to use to illuminate the reasons for individual attitudes toward escalation of the conflict.

Table A.4 presents the results for the model that sought to predict respondents' approval or disapproval of sending troops to better protect the U.S. troops in Somalia, and Table A.5 reports the results of the model that sought to predict respondents' approval or disapproval for continuing to try capturing the warlord Aidid. Our hypothesis is that the willingness to escalate should be associated with the perceived stakes or benefits, the prospects for success, and the likely costs; unfortunately, there was no variable for costs in this dataset, so we estimate the model without one parameter.

Table A.3
Wording of Question in ABC News Somalia Poll, October 5, 1993

Variable	Question Wording
Escalation	Q7. The Clinton administration says it is sending 450 more troops with tanks and other heavy equipment to better protect the U.S. troops who are there now. Do you favor or oppose this move?
	Q8. The Somali fighters are commanded by a warlord named Mohammed Aidid. The United States, along with other United Nations forces, have been sending out its troops to try to capture Aidid. Do you think the United States should continue trying to capture Aidid, or not?
Vital Interests	Q6. Do you think America's vital interests are at stake in Somalia or not?
Prospects	Q10. Just your best guess: Do you think the United States is going to get bogged down in a drawn-out military involvement in Somalia, or do you think the U.S. military involvement there will end quickly?

Table A.4
Marginal Probability from Probit Estimates of Escalation (Q7)

Variables	Change in Probability at Mean Values
Vital interests (q6)[†]	0.135 (0.058)**
Prospects (q10)[†]	0.231 (0.048)***
Party 1 if Republican[†]	0.042 (0.065)
Party 1 if Independent[†]	–0.053 (0.067)
Gender 1 if female[†]	–0.129 (0.052)**
Wald Chi-square (Prod > Chi2)	35.90 (0.000)
Log-likelihood	–263.25612
Observations	413
Correctly specified	64%

SOURCE: ABC News, October 5, 1993. The escalation question was coded as 0 if the respondent did not support sending additional troops to Somalia, and 1 if they supported additional troops.
[†] dF/dx is for discrete change of dummy variable from 0 to 1.
* Significant at 10%.
** Significant at 5%.
*** Significant at 1%.
Robust standard error in parentheses.

Despite the missing costs parameter, the first model correctly predicts 64 percent of the respondents' positions on sending more troops, and the second correctly predicts 60 percent of the cases. Both models suggest that the desire to escalate was associated with a belief in the importance of the stakes, and a belief that the U.S. effort would be successful. The diagnostics for both models also are good.

Table A.5
Marginal Probability from Probit Estimates of Escalation (Q8)

Variables	Change in Probability at Mean Values
Vital interests (q6)[†]	0.128 (0.060)**
Prospects (q10)[†]	0.180 (0.050)***
Party 1 if Republican[†]	−0.039 (0.066)
Party 1 if Independent[†]	−0.081 (0.067)
Gender 1 if female[†]	−0.099 (0.052)*
Wald Chi-square (Prod > Chi2)	22.41 (0.000)
Log-likelihood	−267.06
Observations	404
Correctly specified	60%

SOURCE: ABC News, October 5, 1993. The escalation question was coded as 0 if the respondent did not support additional efforts to capture Aidid, and 1 if they supported such efforts.
[†] dF/dx is for discrete change of dummy variable from 0 to 1.
* Significant at 10%.
** Significant at 5%.
*** Significant at 1%.
Robust standard error in parentheses.

Statistical Results for Haiti

Cross-Tabulations of Support and Independent Variables

As shown in Tables B.1 through B.6, simple Chi-square tests of the association between support for the presence of U.S. troops in Haiti and beliefs about the U.S. stakes in Haiti (both moral interests and more traditional national security interests), prospects for success, expected casualties, and party suggested that support was associated with all four variables, and all were statistically significant at the .001 level.

Table B.1 presents results showing that approval and disapproval of the presence of U.S. troops in Haiti were systematically associated with beliefs about the U.S. moral interests in Haiti, in this case, whether or not the Haitian people would, as a result, be better off as a result of the intervention.

Table B.1
Cross-Tabulation of Support for Presence of U.S. Troops in Haiti and Moral Interests, September 1994

Q15. Do you approve or disapprove of the presence of U.S. troops in Haiti?

Q22. When it comes time for the United States to withdraw its troops from Haiti, do you think the Haitian people will be better off than before the U.S. arrived, worse off, or will their situation not have changed?

	% Approve	% Disapprove	N
Better off	74	26	525
Worse off	38	62	74
Not changed	31	68	395
Don't know/refused	57	16	15
Total	54	45	1,008

SOURCE: Gallup, September 23–25, 1994.
NOTE: p < .001 in a Chi-square test of independence.

Table B.2 presents the results of our cross-tabulation of approval of the presence of U.S. forces in Haiti and the United States' stakes in terms of more national security interests, in this case, the belief that U.S. involvement would lead to a reduction in the flow of Haitian refugees to the United States.

Table B.2
Cross-Tabulation of Support for Presence of U.S. Troops in Haiti and National Security Interests, September 1994

Q15. Do you approve or disapprove of the presence of U.S. troops in Haiti?

Q19. Please tell me whether you think each of the following is likely or not likely to happen in Haiti (as a result of U.S. involvement in that country)... There will be a reduction in the flow of Haitian refuges to the U.S.

	% Approve	% Disapprove	N
Likely	68	31	546
Not likely	38	61	452
Don't know/refused	45	55	9
Total	54	45	1,008

SOURCE: Gallup, September 23–25, 1994.
NOTE: $p < .001$ in a Chi-square test of independence.

Because this is a somewhat imperfect question for estimating the importance of beliefs about the importance of national interests in Haiti, we also present the results of our cross-tabulation of approval for the president's handling of Haiti and the belief that the United States had vital interests at stake in Haiti (Table B.3) from a poll done in October 1993. As suggested by the statistical significance of the Chi-square test result, approval of the president's handling of the situation was associated with the belief that the United States had vital interests in Haiti.

Table B.3
Cross-Tabulation of Approval of the President's Handling of Haiti by Belief in Vital Interests, October 1993

Q3. Do you approve or disapprove of the way Clinton is handling the situation in Haiti?

Q13. Do you think America's vital interests are at stake in Haiti, or not?

	% Approve	% Disapprove	N
Yes	36	45	139
No	28	55	322
No opinion	16	23	43
Total	29	50	504

SOURCE: ABC News, October 12, 1993.
NOTE: $p < 0.001$ in a Chi-square test of independence.

Table B.4 shows that approval and disapproval of the U.S. presence was systematically associated with the level of confidence that U.S. troops would be able to withdraw within a few months as planned.

Table B.4
Cross-Tabulation of Support for Presence of Military Troops in Haiti and Prospects for Success, September 1994

Q15. Do you approve or disapprove of the presence of U.S. troops in Haiti?

Q18b. Regarding the situation in Haiti, how confident are you that most of the U.S. troops will be able to withdraw within a few months as planned

	% Approve	% Disapprove	N
Very confident	74	25	135
Somewhat confident	68	30	382
Not too confident	46	53	315
Not at all confident	22	77	164
Don't know/refused	36	64	11
Total	54	45	1,008

SOURCE: Gallup, September 23–25, 1994.
NOTE: $p < .001$ in a Chi-square test of independence.

Table B.5 shows that approval and disapproval of the U.S. presence was associated with the level of confidence that the United States would be able to accomplish its objectives with very few or no casualties.

Table B.5
Cross-Tabulation of Support for Presence of Military Troops in Haiti and Expected Casualties, September 1994

Q15. Do you approve or disapprove of the presence of U.S. troops in Haiti?

Q18a. Regarding the situation in Haiti, how confident are you that the U.S. will be able to accomplish its goals with very few or no American casualties

	% Approve	% Disapprove	N
Very confident	74	24	192
Somewhat confident	68	31	375
Not too confident	40	59	284
Not at all confident	19	81	138
Don't know/refused	42	52	19
Total	54	45	1,008

SOURCE: Gallup, September 23–25, 1994.
NOTE: $p < .001$ in a Chi-square test of independence.

Table B.6 presents the results of a cross-tabulation of approval or disapproval of the presence of U.S. troops in Haiti by party and self-reported consumption of information on Haiti. The hypothesis is that the more information about Haiti a respondent was exposed to, the closer his/her position would be to his/her natural, partisan leaders.[1]

---

[1]In technical terms, the hypothesis in fact is just the opposite: that support is not related to party and information, and the test aims to falsify this hypothesis.

Table B.6
Cross-Tabulation of Support for Presence of Military Troops in Haiti, Party Affiliation, and Consumption of Information, September 1994

Q15. Do you approve or disapprove of the presence of U.S. troops in Haiti?

Q14. As you may know, the military leaders of Haiti have agreed to step down from power by October 15th and President Clinton has sent U.S. troops into Haiti to enforce this agreement. How closely have you been following this situation in Haiti?

Republicans:	% Approve	% Disapprove	N
Closely	40	59	97
Somewhat closely	50	50	153
Not closely	39	58	63
Total	45	54	314

Democrats:	% Approve	% Disapprove	N
Very closely	76	23	102
Somewhat closely	70	30	144
Not closely	59	36	58
Total	70	29	303

Independents:	% Approve	% Disapprove	N
Very closely	57	43	110
Somewhat closely	47	52	157
Not closely	43	54	97
Total	49	49	364

SOURCE: Gallup, September 23–25, 1994.
NOTE: $p < 0.125$ (Republicans), $p < 0.024$ (Democrats), $p < 0.030$ (Independents), in a Chi-square test of independence.

The results in the table confirm this result for Democrats—those who were following Haiti most closely were also most likely to follow the president's lead. It also suggests that Independents generally also were following the president's lead; the results are inconclusive for Republicans, however—there is no clear pattern to Republicans' response, and as a result, they fail to achieve statistical significance.

Cross-Tabulations of Independent Variables and Party

The beliefs that the United States had security interests (as proxied by the belief that there would be a reduction in the flow of Haitian refugees as a result of U.S. involvement in Haiti, Table B.7) or moral interests (as proxied by the belief that Haitians would be better off as a result of the U.S. involvement, Table B.8) in Haiti were associated with party, achieving statistically significant results in both cases.

Table B.7
Cross-Tabulation of Security Interests in Haiti and Party, September 1994

Q19. Please tell me whether you think each of the following is likely or not likely to happen in Haiti (as a result of U.S. involvement in that country)

b. There will be a reduction in the flow of Haitian refugees to the U.S.

	% Likely	% Not Likely	N
Republican	47	52	314
Democrat	66	34	303
Independent	51	47	364
Other	34	66	5
Don't know/refused	49	51	22
Total	54	45	1,008

SOURCE: Gallup, September 23–25, 1994.
NOTE: $p < 0.0024$ in a Chi-square test of independence.

Table B.8
Cross-Tabulation of Moral Interests in Haiti and Party, September 1994

Q22. When it comes time for the United States to withdraw its troops from Haiti, do you think the Haitian people will be better off than before the U.S. arrived, worse off, or will their situation not have changed?

In politics, as of today, do you consider yourself a Republican, a Democrat, or Independent?

	% Better off	% Worse off	% Not changed	N
Republican	48	6	44	314
Democrat	64	8	27	303
Independent	48	7	44	364
Other	13	17	70	5
Don't know/refused	24	17	47	22
Total	52	7	39	1,008

SOURCE: Gallup, September 23–25, 1994.
NOTE: $p < .001$ in a Chi-square test of independence.

Confidence that the United States would achieve its objectives and be able to withdraw in a few months as planned (Table B.9) and expectations regarding casualties (Table B.10) were also associated with party orientation, with the result statistically significant in both cases; there was not a statistically significant relationship between information consumption and party.

Table B.9
Cross-Tabulation of Expected Length of the Campaign in Haiti by Party, September 1994

Q18b. Regarding the situation in Haiti, how confident are you that most of the U.S. troops will be able to withdraw within a few month as planned

In politics, as of today, do you consider yourself a Republican, a Democrat or Independent?

	% Very confident	% Somewhat confident	% Not too confident	% Not at all confident	N
Republican	9	29	39	22	314
Democrat	18	47	27	8	303
Independent	14	38	29	17	364
Other	17	13	21	49	5
Don't know/refused	4	37	24	27	22
Total	13	38	31	16	1,008

SOURCE: Gallup, September 23–25, 1994.
NOTE: p < .001 in a Chi-square test of independence.

Table B.10
Cross-Tabulation of Expected Casualties in Haiti and Party, September 1994

Q18a. Regarding the situation in Haiti, how confident are you that the U.S. will be able to accomplish its goals with very few or no American casualties?

In politics, as of today, do you consider yourself a Republican, a Democrat or Independent?

	% Very confident	% Somewhat confident	% Not too confident	% Not at all confident	N
Republican	15	34	32	17	314
Democrat	25	43	23	7	303
Independent	18	37	29	15	364
Other	17	0	21	49	5
Don't know/refused	17	14	42	19	22
Total	19	37	28	14	1,008

SOURCE: Gallup, September 23–25, 1994.
NOTE: p < .001 in a Chi-square test of independence.

As shown in Table B.11, news followership was not statistically associated with party.

Table B.11
Cross-Tabulation of News Consumption Regarding Haiti and Party, September 1994

Q14. As you may know, the military leaders of Haiti have agreed to step down from power by October 15th and President Clinton has sent U.S. troops into Haiti to enforce this agreement. How closely have you been following this situation in Haiti?

In politics, as of today, do you consider yourself a Republican, a Democrat or Independent?

	% Very closely	% Somewhat closely	% Not too closely	% Not closely at all	N
Republican	31	49	15	5	314
Democrat	34	47	14	5	303
Independent	30	43	20	7	364
Other	0	74	13	12	5
Don't know/refused	34	33	22	11	22
Total	31	46	17	6	1,008

SOURCE: Gallup, September 23–25, 1994.
NOTE: $p < 0.7140$ in a Chi-square test of independence.

Results of Statistical Modeling

Table B.12 presents the wording of the questions used in our statistical modeling.

Table B.12
Wording of Questions in Gallup/CNN/USA Today Poll, September 23–25 1994

Variable	Question Wording
Support	Q15. Do you approve or disapprove of the presence of U.S. troops in Haiti?
Security interests	Q19b. Please tell me whether you think each of the following is likely or not likely to happen in Haiti (as a result of U.S. Involvement in that country): There will be a reduction in the flow of Haitian refuges to the U.S.
Moral interests	Q22. When it comes time for the United States to withdraw its troops from Haiti, do you think the Haitian people will be better off than before the U.S. arrived, worse off, or will their situation not have changed? 0-1-2 categorical scale.
Prospects	Q18b. Regarding the situation in Haiti, how confident are you that most of the U.S. troops will be able to withdraw within a few month as planned? 0-1-2-3 categorical scale.
Costs	Q18a. Regarding the situation in Haiti, how confident are you that the U.S. will be able to accomplish its goals with very few or no American casualties? 0-1-2-3 categorical scale.
Information	Q14. As you may know, the military leaders of Haiti have agreed to step down from power by October 15th and President Clinton has sent U.S. troops into Haiti to enforce this agreement. How closely have you been following this situation in Haiti?

We included all of the covariates (e.g., race, gender, and education) that we believed might also have an effect, in order to be able to claim that the coefficients represent possible change in support keeping all else constant.

Table B.13 presents the results of our "best" model, i.e., the model that used questions that seemed to be the best fit for the concepts of stakes or benefits, prospects for success, and costs.

Table B.13
Marginal Probability from the Probit Estimates of Approval (Q15)

Variables	Change in Probability at Mean Values
Moral Interests (Q22)	0.238 (0.036)***
Security Interests (q19b)[†]	0.173 (0.040)***
Prospects (q18b)	0.084 (0.026)***
Casualties (q18a)	–0.124 (0.026)***
Party 1 if Republican[†]	–0.167 (0.053)***
Party 1 if Independent[†]	–0.173 (0.050)***
Information (q14)	0.035 (0.026)
Race 1 if Black[†]	0.113 (0.075)
Gender 1 if female[†]	–0.059 (0.040)
Wald Chi-square (Prod > Chi2)	207.02 (0.000)
Log-likelihood	–501.30
Observations	964
Correctly specified	75%

SOURCE: Gallup, September 23–25, 1994.
[†] dF/dx is for discrete change of dummy variable from 0 to 1.
* Significant at 10%.
** Significant at 5%.
*** Significant at 1%.
Robust standard error in parentheses.

As the results in the table suggest, our model was able to correctly classify 75 percent of the respondents in terms of whether they approved or disapproved of the presence of U.S. troops in Haiti, and beliefs in moral and security interests, the prospects for success, casualties, and party were all significant in the regression.

The coefficients (the probability of support given an increase in the independent variable) suggest that a belief that the United States had moral or security interests in Haiti and whether the respondent was a member of the president's party (i.e., Democrat) were the most important factors conditioning whether or not the respondent approved of the presence of U.S. troops in Haiti. Next most important were beliefs that the casualties would be low and, finally, that the prospects for success were good.

None of the other variables or interaction effects we tested (e.g., between party and information consumption) in the multivariate model proved significant, and they did not increase the explanatory power of the model.

Statistical Results for Bosnia

Cross-Tabulations of Support and Independent Variables

Our cross-tabulation of support for contributing U.S. troops to an international peacekeeping force and beliefs that the United States needed to be involved in Bosnia in order to protect its own interests (Table C.1) showed that a belief that the United States had important security interests in Bosnia was associated with support for the U.S. troops, with the results statistically significant at the .001 level.

Table C.1
Cross-Tabulation of Support for Military Troops in Bosnia and Beliefs About Security Interests, November 1995

Q2. Now that a peace agreement has been reached by all the groups currently fighting in Bosnia, the Clinton administration plans to contribute U.S. troops to an international peacekeeping force. Do you favor or oppose that?

Q4. Do you think the United States needs to be involved in Bosnia in order to protect its own interests, or don't you think so?

	% Favor	% Oppose	N
Needs to be involved	75	11	225
Don't think so	26	67	333
Don't know/refused	50	5	77
Total	46	40	635

SOURCE: Gallup, November 27, 1995.
NOTE: p < .001 in a Chi-square test of independence.

In a similar vein, the belief that the United States had a moral obligation to help keep the peace in Bosnia was associated with support for contributing troops (Table C.2), and the results again were statistically significant at the .001 level.

Table C.2
Cross-Tabulation of Support for Military Troops in Bosnia and Belief in U.S. Moral Obligation, November 1995

Q2. Now that a peace agreement has been reached by all the groups currently fighting in Bosnia, the Clinton administration plans to contribute U.S. troops to an international peacekeeping force? Do you favor or oppose that?

Q7. Do you think the United States has a moral obligation to help keep the peace in Bosnia, or not?

	% Favor	% Oppose	N
Yes, does have moral obligations	68	20	338
No, does not	21	68	256
Don't know/refused	24	32	41
Total	46	40	635

SOURCE: Gallup, November 27, 1995.
NOTE: p < .001 in a Chi-square test of independence.

Support for contributing troops also was positively associated with the belief that the United States had good prospects—as measured by respondents' confidence in the president's ability to handle the situation in Bosnia (Table C.3)—again, at the .001 level of statistical significance.

Table C.3
Cross-Tabulation of Support for Military Troops in Bosnia and Confidence in Ability to Handle Situation (in Percentage and Number of Observation), November 1995

Q2. Now that a peace agreement has been reached by all the groups currently fighting in Bosnia, the Clinton administration plans to contribute U.S. troops to an international peacekeeping force. Do you favor or oppose that?

Q5. How confident are you in President Clinton's ability to handle the situation in Bosnia?

	% Favor	% Oppose	N
Very confident	76	16	131
Somewhat confident	58	27	267
Not too confident	25	61	122
Not at all confident	7	78	96
Don't know/refused	10	57	19
Total	46	40	635

SOURCE: Gallup, November 27, 1995.
NOTE: p < .001 in a Chi-square test of independence.

Support also was negatively associated with the belief that the commitment in Bosnia was likely to be a long-term one involving many casualties (see Table C.4), again at the .001 level of significance.

Table C.4
Cross-Tabulation of Support for Military Troops in Bosnia and Expected Length of Commitment and Number of Casualties, November 1995

Q2. Now that a peace agreement has been reached by all the groups currently fighting in Bosnia, the Clinton administration plans to contribute U.S. troops to an international peacekeeping force. Do you favor or oppose that?

Q9. If the United States sends troops as part of a peacekeeping mission, do you think that is likely to lead to a long-term commitment in Bosnia involving many casualties, or not?

	% Favor	% Oppose	N
Yes, likely to lead to long-term commitment	32	58	338
No, not likely	72	17	221
Don't know/refused	36	24	76
Total	46	40	635

SOURCE: Gallup, November 27, 1995.
NOTE: $p < .001$ in a Chi-square test of independence.

Support for contributing troops also was associated with individuals' level of confidence regarding their leaders' ability to handle the situation in Bosnia (Table C.5);[2] those who had greater confidence in the president were more inclined to support the policy of intervention, and those who had greater confidence in Republican leaders tended to oppose it.

Table C.5
Support for Military Troops in Bosnia by Confidence in Party Leaders, November 1995

Q2. Now that a peace agreement has been reached by all the groups currently fighting in Bosnia, the Clinton administration plans to contribute U.S. troops to an international peacekeeping force. Do you favor or oppose that?

Q6. Who do you have more confidence in when it comes to handling the situation in Bosnia: President Clinton or the Republican leaders in Congress?

	% Favor	% Oppose	N
President Clinton	61	26	329
Republican leaders in Congress	28	58	173
Neither/both/mixed	31	61	79
Don't know/refused	36	37	54
Total	46	40	635

SOURCE: Gallup, November 27, 1995.
NOTE: $p < .001$ in a Chi-square test of independence.

Cross-Tabulations of Independent Variables and Party

The belief that the United States had important stakes in Bosnia, whether in terms of security interests (Table C.6) or in terms of a moral obligation to help keep the peace (Table C.7), was associated with confidence in party leaders, our proxy for party, and this result was statistically significant.

---

[2]We use this variable because the poll did not ask respondents to identify their party.

Table C.6
Cross-Tabulation of Beliefs About Security Interests in Bosnia and Expected Length of Commitment Involving Casualties (in Percentage and Number of Observations), November 1995

Q4. Do you think the United States needs to be involved in Bosnia in order to protect its own interests, or don't you think so?

Q6. Who do you have more confidence in when it comes to handling the situation in Bosnia: President Clinton or the Republican leaders in Congress?

	% Needs to be involved	% Don't think so	N
Clinton	49	41	329
Republicans	22	66	173
Both/None	21	68	79
Don't know/refused	18	54	54
Total	35	52	635

SOURCE: Gallup, November 27, 1995.
NOTE: p < .001 in a Chi-square test of independence.

Table C.7
Cross-Tabulation of Beliefs in Moral Obligations by Confidence in Party Leaders (in Percentage and Number of Observation), November 1995

Q7. Do you think the United States has moral obligations to help keep the peace in Bosnia, or not?

Q6. Who do you have more confidence in when it comes to handling the situation in Bosnia: President Clinton or the Republican leaders in Congress?

	Yes, does have moral obligations	No, does not	N
Clinton	65	30	329
Republicans	37	58	173
Both/None	49	46	79
Don't know/refused	38	40	54
Total	53	40	635

SOURCE: Gallup, November 27, 1995.
NOTE: p < .001 in a Chi-square test of independence.

The perceived prospects for success, as measured by confidence in the president's ability to handle the situation in Bosnia (Table C.8) and the belief that the commitment would be a long-term one with many casualties (Table C.9), were also associated with our proxy for party, and these results were statistically significant.

Table C.8

Cross-Tabulation of Confidence in President's Ability to Handle Situation in Bosnia by Confidence in Party Leaders (in Percentage and Number of Observations), November 1995

Q5. How confident are you in President Clinton's ability to handle the situation in Bosnia?

Q6. Who do you have more confidence in when it comes to handling the situation in Bosnia: President Clinton or the Republican leaders in Congress?

	% Very confident	% Somewhat confident	% Not too confident	% Not at all confident	N
Clinton	36	53	9	2	329
Republicans	1	28	35	36	173
Both/none	7	30	28	31	79
Don't know/refused	12	43	21	9	54
Total	21	42	19	15	635

SOURCE: Gallup, November 27, 1995.
NOTE: p < .001 in a Chi-square test of independence.

Table C.9

Cross-Tabulation of Expected Length of Commitment and Expected Casualties in Bosnia by Confidence in Party Leaders (in Percentage and Number of Observation), November 1995

Q9. If the United States sends troops as part of a peacekeeping mission, do you think that is likely to lead to a long-term commitment in Bosnia involving many casualties, or not?

Q6. Who do you have more confidence in when it comes to handling the situation in Bosnia: President Clinton or the Republican leaders in Congress?

	% Yes, likely to lead to long-term commitment	% No, not likely	N
Clinton	40	49	329
Republicans	75	18	173
Both/none	68	20	79
Don't know/refused	39	26	54
Total	53	35	635

SOURCE: Gallup, November 27, 1995.
NOTE: p < .001 in a Chi-square test of independence.

Results of Statistical Modeling

There were several challenges with this dataset we encountered in estimating a model of support. First, the prospects for success were proxied by a question about the president's ability to handle situation. Moreover, the questionnaire did not ask about party identification, so party was proxied by a question that asked who the respondent had higher confidence in with respect to situation in Bosnia—the President (a Democrat), or members of the Republican majority in the Congress. The wording of the questions used is presented in Table C.10.

Table C.10
Wording of Question in Gallup/CNN/USA Today Poll: Bosnia Speech, November 27, 1995

Variable	Wording of Question
Support	Q2. Now that a peace agreement has been reached by all the groups currently fighting in Bosnia, the Clinton administration plans to contribute U.S. troops to an international peacekeeping force. Do you favor or oppose that?
Benefits	Q4. Do you think the United States needs to be involved in Bosnia in order to protect its own interests, or don't you think so?
	Q7. Do you think the United States has moral obligations to help keep the peace in Bosnia, or not?
Prospects	Q5. How confident are you in President Clinton's ability to handle the situation in Bosnia?
Costs	Q9. If the United States sends troops as part of a peacekeeping mission, do you think that is likely to lead to a long-term commitment in Bosnia involving many casualties, or not?
Proxy for party	Q6. Who do you have more confidence in when it comes to handling the situation in Bosnia: President Clinton or the Republican leaders in Congress?

SOURCE: Gallup, October 27, 1995.

Notwithstanding these technical issues, the benefits-prospects-costs paradigm proved quite good in explaining covariance patterns in the support for the military campaign in Bosnia: the model correctly predicted over 80 percent of the respondents in terms of whether they favored or opposed contributing U.S. troops to an international peacekeeping force in Bosnia (Table C.11); the second column of coefficients is for the full model, while the first column is for the reduced-form model.

From the table we can see that the most important factor in determining support was the perception of security interests, the next most important factor was respondents' beliefs about whether the costs in casualties were likely to be high, the third was the perception of moral interests, and the fourth was the belief that a successful outcome was likely; although party was a statistically significant predictor on a bivariate basis, it proved not to be significant in this model, possibly the result of the imperfect proxy we used.

The reduced-form models for Bosnia also suggested that the theoretically important variables were the critical ones: support or opposition to Bosnia could be predicted for 82 percent of the respondents by knowing only their beliefs about the stakes, prospects for success, and expected costs; including party and information consumption raised it to 83 percent.

Table C.11
Marginal Probability from the Probit Estimates of Approval (Q2)

Variables	Change in Probability at Mean Values	Change in Probability at Mean Values
Security interests (Q4)[†]	0.332 (0.064)***	0.334 (0.064)***
Moral interests (q7)[†]	0.273 (0.068)***	0.280 (0.068)***
Prospects (q5)	0.197 (0.044)***	0.198 (0.045)***
Casualties (q9)[†]	−0.274 (0.063)***	−0.273 (0.063)***
Party 1 if Republican[†]	−0.011 (0.079)	−0.008 (0.078)
Race 1 if black[†]	0.032 (0.119)	0.029 (0.120)
Gender 1 if female[†]	0.054 (0.068)	0.057 (0.070)
Education 1 if high school[†]		−0.026 (0.132)
Education 1 if some college[†]		0.005 (0.129)
Education 1 if college graduate[†]		−0.018 (0.142)
Education 1 if postgraduate[†]		−0.118 (0.130)
Wald Chi-square (Prod > Chi2)	128.06 (0.000)	147.58 (0.000)
Log-likelihood	−191.79	−190.88
Observations	468	468
Correctly specified	83%	84%

SOURCE: Gallup, November 27, 1995.
[†] dF/dx is for discrete change of dummy variable from 0 to 1.
* Significant at 10%.
** Significant at 5%
*** Significant at 1%.
Robust standard error in parentheses.

Statistical Results for Kosovo

There were two datasets from the Kosovo campaign that asked all of the questions needed to test our model: Pew Research Center, April 15–18, 1999, and Pew Research Center, May 12–16, 1999. The two questionnaires were conducted by the same agency and used consistent question wording, which allows us not only to test the model itself, but also to determine how efficiently results from the regression in one dataset can be used to predict support in the other. For each dataset, we first present bivariate tabulations of the main variables used in the analysis, then the results of the logistic regression analysis.

Cross-Tabulations of Support and Independent Variables

We first present cross tabulations and Chi-square tests of independence of support for ground troops in Kosovo with beliefs about the nature of the stakes involved, the expected length of the campaign, and the expected casualties and financial costs. In all cases, the association between support and the independent variables was statistically significant at the 0.001 level.

Results in Table D.1 suggest that approval for sending U.S. ground troops to Kosovo was systematically associated with the belief that the United States had moral interests in Kosovo; preventing the killing of citizens of Kosovo was seen as an important justification for the campaign and was associated with support in a statistically significant way.

Table D.1
Cross-Tabulation of Support for Sending U.S. Ground Troops to Kosovo and Moral Interests, April 1999

Q8. If the air strikes do not stop Serbian military attacks in Kosovo, would you favor or oppose sending U.S. ground troops to Kosovo along with troops from other NATO countries?

Q16. Here are some reasons being given for using U.S. troops to help secure peace in Kosovo, Serbia. For each one, please tell me whether, in your opinion, it is a very important reason, a somewhat important reason, a not too important reason, or not at all important reason for the use of U.S. troops.

b. to prevent the killing of citizens in Kosovo:

	% Favor	% Oppose	N
Very important	54	41	353
Somewhat important	37	61	94
Not too important	11	86	24
Not at all important	14	74	25
Don't know/refused	37	23	6
Total	47	48	502

SOURCE: Pew, April 15–18, 1999.
NOTE: $p < .001$ in a Chi-square test of independence.

Table D.2 presents results of a cross-tabulation of support with the level of concern that U.S. troops might be in Kosovo for a long time, and suggests that the level of approval for the campaign was associated with such concerns.

Table D.2
Cross-Tabulation of Support for Sending U.S. Ground Troops to Kosovo and Prospects for Success, April 1999

Q8. If the air strikes do not stop Serbian military attacks in Kosovo, would you favor or oppose sending U.S. ground troops to Kosovo along with troops from other NATO countries?

Q17c. How worried are you that U.S. troops could be involved in Kosovo for a long time: very worried, somewhat worried, not too worried, or not at all worried?

	% Favor	% Oppose	N
Very worried	39	57	313
Somewhat worried	56	37	125
Not too worried	70	24	46
Not at all worried	58	32	16
Don't know/refused	43	57	1
Total	47	48	502

SOURCE: Pew, April 15–18, 1999.
NOTE: $p < .001$ in a Chi-square test of independence.

Table D.3 shows that support for sending U.S. ground troops to Kosovo was associated with concerns about expected casualties; those who were most concerned also were the most likely to oppose sending troops.

Table D.3
Cross-Tabulation of Approval for Sending U.S. Ground Troops to Kosovo and Worries About Expected Casualties, April 1999

Q8. If the air strikes do not stop Serbian military attacks in Kosovo, would you favor or oppose sending U.S. ground troops to Kosovo along with troops from other NATO countries?

Q17a. How worried are you that U.S. troops in Kosovo might suffer casualties: very worried, somewhat worried, not too worried, or not at all worried?

	% Favor	% Oppose	N
Very worried	41	54	331
Somewhat worried	59	37	127
Not too worried	64	29	26
Not at all worried	38	62	15
Don't know/refused	0	0	3
Total	47	48	502

SOURCE: Pew, April 15–18, 1999.
NOTE: $p < .001$ in a Chi-square test of independence.

In addition, Table D.4 suggests that support for sending U.S. ground troops to Kosovo was associated with expected financial costs of the campaign.

Table D.4
Cross-Tabulation of Support for Sending U.S. Ground Troops to Kosovo and Expected Financial Costs of the Campaign, April 1999

Q8. If the air strikes do not stop Serbian military attacks in Kosovo, would you favor or oppose sending U.S. ground troops to Kosovo along with troops from other NATO countries?

Q17b. How worried are you about the financial costs of sending U.S. troops to Kosovo: very worried, somewhat worried, not too worried, or not at all worried?

	% Favor	% Oppose	N
Very worried	36	60	193
Somewhat worried	44	48	175
Not too worried	65	33	79
Not at all worried	65	30	55
Don't know/refused	0	100	1
Total	47	48	502

SOURCE: Pew, April 15–18, 1999.
NOTE: $p < 0.001$ in a Chi-square test of independence.

Table D.5 presents the results of a cross-tabulation of whether individuals favor or oppose sending U.S. ground troops to Kosovo by party and self-reported consumption of information about situation in Kosovo; as shown, there was a statistically significant relationship between party information for Democrats and Republicans, but not for Independents.

Table D.5
Cross-Tabulation of Support for Sending U.S. Ground Troops to Kosovo and Party Information, April 1999

Q8. If the air strikes do not stop Serbian military attacks in Kosovo, would you favor or oppose sending U.S. ground troops to Kosovo along with troops from other NATO countries?

Q4. Now I will read a list of some stories covered by news organizations this past month. As I read each item, tell me if you happened to follow this news story very closely, fairly closely, not too closely, or not at all closely?

b. The capture of three U.S. soldiers near Kosovo, Serbia.

Democrats:	% Favor	% Oppose	N
Closely	56	40	133
Not closely	35	65	33
Total	52	45	167
Republicans:	% Favor	% Oppose	N
Closely	49	47	133
Not closely	18	60	16
Total	46	48	149
Independents:	% Favor	% Oppose	N
Closely	44	51	139
Not closely	39	49	15
Total	43	51	154

SOURCE: Pew, April 15–18, 1999.
NOTE: $p < 0.0321$ (Democrats), $p < 0.0028$ (Republicans), $p < 0.6627$ (Independent), in a Chi-square test of independence.

Cross-Tabulation of Independent Variables and Party

Table D.6 suggests that member of the President's party were more likely to favor sending U.S. ground troops to Kosovo than others.

Table D.6
Cross-Tabulation of Support for Ground Troops in Kosovo by Party, April 1999

Q8. If the air strikes do not stop Serbian military attacks in Kosovo, would you favor or oppose sending U.S. ground troops to Kosovo along with troops from other NATO countries?

D7. In politics today, do you consider yourself a Republican, Democrat, or Independent?

	Approve	Disapprove	N
Republican	46	48	149
Democrat	52	45	167
Independent	43	51	154
No preference	36	55	23
Don't know/refused	33	35	9
Total	47	48	502

SOURCE: Pew, April 15–18, 1999.
NOTE: $p < 0.0491$ in a Chi-square test of independence.

As it often is the case that party leadership influences not only support for the campaign, but also the strength of beliefs about stakes, prospects and expected casualties, the next several tables present cross-tabulation of beliefs about stakes, prospects and costs by party.

Tables D.7 and D.8 show that although roughly the same percentages of Republicans and Democrats thought preventing the killings in Kosovo to be at least somewhat important, they differed in the intensity of the importance they ascribed to that goal. For example, Table D.7 suggests that members of the Republican Party (the President's natural opposition party) were less likely to think that preventing killing of people in Kosovo was a very important reason for war than Democrats or Independents.

Table D.7
Cross-Tabulation of the Stakes of the Campaign in Kosovo by Party, April 1999

Q16. Here are some reasons being given for using U.S. troops to help secure peace in Kosovo, Serbia. For each one, please tell me whether, in your opinion, it is a very important reason, a somewhat important reason, a not too important reason, or not at all important reason for the use of U.S. troops.

b. To prevent the killing of citizens in Kosovo.

D7. In politics today, do you consider yourself a Republican, Democrat, or Independent?

	Very important	Somewhat important	Not too important	Not at all important	N
Republican	63	24	8	4	271
Democrat	74	16	5	4	350
Independent	70	17	5	6	308
No preference	65	16	10	5	58
Don't know/refused	43	17	12	16	14
Total	69	19	6	5	1,000

SOURCE: Pew, April 15–18, 1999.
NOTE: $p < 0.005$ in a Chi-square test of independence.

From Table D.8 we can see that those respondents who considered themselves a member of the Democratic party were less likely to be very worried that U.S. troops would be in Kosovo for a long time.

Table D.8
Cross-Tabulation of the Prospects for Success by Party, April 1999

Q17c. How worried are you that U.S. troops could be involved in Kosovo for a long time: very worried, somewhat worried, not too worried, or not at all worried?

D7. In politics today, do you consider yourself a Republican, Democrat, or Independent?

	Very worried	Somewhat worried	Not too worried	Not at all worried	N
Republican	68	21	10	1	149
Democrat	59	30	7	3	167
Independent	61	23	10	5	154
No preference	68	22	10	0	23
Don't know/refused	33	26	14	17	9
Total	62	25	9	3	502

SOURCE: Pew, April 15–18, 1999.
NOTE: $p < 0.005$ in a Chi-square test of independence.

A similar pattern holds for the beliefs about casualties (Table D.9). Those respondents who were members of the Democratic Party were less likely to say that they are very worried about possible casualties (most were somewhat worried). So in many cases it is a matter of degree: most respondents were concerned with possible casualties.

Table D.9
Cross-Tabulation of the Expectation of the Casualties in Kosovo by Party, April 1999

Q17a. How worried are you that U.S. troops in Kosovo might suffer casualties: very worried, somewhat worried, not too worried, or not at all worried?

D7. In politics today, do you consider yourself a Republican, Democrat, or Independent?

	Very worried	Somewhat worried	Not too worried	Not at all worried	N
Republican	72	22	4	2	149
Democrat	62	29	5	4	167
Independent	67	23	6	2	154
No preference	63	28	0	9	23
Don't know/refused	36	50	14	0	9
Total	66	25	5	3	502

SOURCE: Pew, April 15–18, 1999.
NOTE: p < 0.4492 in a Chi-square test of independence.

Results of Statistical Modeling

Results of the cross-tabulations suggested that there was some association between the main variables of interest: perceptions of stakes, prospects for success, casualties and other costs, and party and information consumption. At the same time, we are more interested in knowing if this association stands up when we use all of these variables together. Table D.10 presents the wording of questions that were used in the logistic regression.

Table D.11 presents the results from the logistic regression. Using this dataset, our model correctly predicted approval or disapproval for 66 percent (for the two reduced-form models) to 73 percent of the respondents (for the full model).

As shown, the belief that the United States had moral interests was the most important factor in predicting support, followed by race, beliefs about the prospects for success, party, information consumption, and financial costs. We can see that concern about casualties was negatively correlated with the probability of support, but not significantly so; this might be explained by the fact that ground troops were not involved in a combat role in the campaign, since at that time, air strikes were the most important part of the campaign.

Table D.10
Wording of Question in Pew Research Center for the People and the Press April 1999 News Interest Index, April 15–18 1999.

Variable	Description
Support	Q8. Form 1. If the air strikes do not stop Serbian military attacks in Kosovo, would you favor or oppose sending U.S. ground troops to Kosovo along with troops from other NATO countries?
Moral interests	Q16b. Here are some reasons being given for using U.S. troops to help secure peace in Kosovo, Serbia. For each one, please tell me whether, in your opinion, it is a very important reason, a somewhat important reason, a not too important reason, or not at all important reason for the use of U.S. troops.
	b. to prevent the killing of citizens in Kosovo
Prospects	Q17c. How worried are you that U.S. troops could be involved in Kosovo for a long time: very worried, somewhat worried, not too worried, or not at all worried?
Casualties	Q17a. How worried are you that U.S. troops in Kosovo might suffer casualties: very worried, somewhat worried, not too worried, or not at all worried?
Financial costs	Q17b. How worried are you about the financial costs of sending U.S. troops to Kosovo — very worried, somewhat worried, not too worried, or not at all worried?
Information	Q4b. Now I will read a list of some stories covered by news organizations this past month. As I read each item, tell me if you happened to follow this news story very closely, fairly closely, not too closely, or not at all closely?
	b. The capture of three U.S. soldiers near Kosovo, Serbia

Table D.11
Marginal Probability from the Probit Estimates of Approval (Q8)

Variable	Change in Probability at Mean Values	Change in Probability at Mean Values	Change in Probability at Mean Values
Benefits (Q16b)	0.183 (0.037)***	0.191 (0.038)***	0.185 (0.038)***
Prospects (q17c)	0.107 (0.040)***	0.130 (0.038)***	0.104 (0.041)**
Casualties (q17a)	−0.040 (0.045)	−0.051 (0.044)	−0.043 (0.046)
Financial costs (q17b)	−0.068 (0.028)**		−0.066 (0.029)**
Party 1 if Republican[†]	−0.062 (0.066)	−0.068 (0.065)	−0.068 (0.067)
Party 1 if Independent[†]	−0.112 (0.065)*	−0.121 (0.064)*	−0.109 (0.065)*
Information consumption (q4b)	0.093 (0.034)***	0.094 (0.034)***	0.089 (0.035)**
Race 1 if Black[†]	−0.199 (0.077)***	−0.207 (0.075)***	−0.191 (0.079)**
Gender 1 if female[†]	−0.032 (0.054)	−0.036 (0.054)	−0.028 (0.055)
Education 1 if less than high school[†]			−0.052 (0.095)
Education 1 if some college[†]			0.041 (0.069)
Education 1 if college graduate[†]			0.005 (0.074)
Education 1 if post graduate[†]			0.075 (0.092)
Income			0.006 (0.015)

Table D.11 (continued)

Variable	Change in Probability at Mean Values	Change in Probability at Mean Values	Change in Probability at Mean Values
Wald Chi-square (Prod > Chi2)	63.69 (0.000)	58.88 (0.000)	68.40 (0.000)
Log-likelihood	−278.57	−282.65	−277.34
Observations	464	464	464
Correctly specified	66%	66%	66%

† dF/dx is for discrete change of dummy variable from 0 to 1.
* Significant at 10%.
** Significant at 5%.
*** Significant at 1%.
Robust standard error in parentheses.

Using the reduced-form models, we were able to correctly predict support or opposition for 64 percent of the respondents using beliefs about the importance of the stakes, prospects for success, and likely casualties, and 66 percent when we also included party and information consumption.

At the same time, we were interested to determine how well this model could predict support in the other dataset, which came from a poll that was conducted one month later (Pew, May 12–16, 1999). Using individual-level data from that poll and estimated coefficients from Table D.11, we predicted support for the campaign, then this prediction with the actual response. Sixty-eight percent of the cases were correctly classified by our model (higher even than in the original dataset).

Statistical Results for Afghanistan

There were several datasets that asked some combination of questions that could be used to estimate the model of support for the global war on terrorism: ABC News/Washington Post September 20, 2001; CBS News, October 8, 2001; and ABC News/Washington Post, November 27, 2001. Here we report the results of the ABC News/Washington Post November 27 poll; the other datasets generally returned similar results.

Cross-Tabulations of Support and Independent Variables

The results in Table E.1 suggest that support for the military action in Afghanistan was associated with perception of benefits of the campaign in a statistically significant manner. In this case, benefits are proxied by a variable that the importance of the U.S. role in the fight against terrorist groups in Afghanistan.

Table E.1
Cross-Tabulation of Support for Military Action In Afghanistan and Interests, November 2001

2. Do you support or oppose the U.S. military action in Afghanistan?

8. When it comes to (READ ITEM), do you think the United States should take the leading role, a large role but not the lead, a lesser role, or no role at all?

d. Taking military action against terrorist groups that try to reestablish themselves in Afghanistan

	% Support	% Oppose	N
Leading role	95	5	414
Large role, but not the lead	93	5	247
Lesser role	77	17	62
No role at all	51	41	23
Don't know/refused	70	6	13
Total	91	7	759

SOURCE: ABC News/Washington Post, November 27, 2001.
NOTE: $p < 0.001$ in a Chi-square test of independence.

Table E.2 presents a cross-tabulation of support for the military action in Afghanistan with an evaluation of how well the campaign is going; support is systematically associated with respondents' favorable assessments of the prospects for the campaign.

Table E.2
Cross-Tabulation of Support for Military Action in Afghanistan and Prospects of the Campaign,
November 2001

Q2. Do you support or oppose the U.S. military action in Afghanistan?

Q5. Do you think the U.S. military action in Afghanistan is going very well, fairly well, not too well or not well at all?

	% Support	% Oppose	N
Very well	97	3	318
Fairly well	92	6	384
Not too well	53	31	24
Not well at all	22	54	13
Don't know/refused	49	30	19
Total	91	7	759

SOURCE: ABC News/Washington Post, November 27, 2001.
NOTE: p < 0.001 in a Chi-square test of independence.

Table E.3 suggests that support for the military action in Afghanistan was significantly associated with expected casualties: those who expected a larger number of casualties were less likely to support the campaign.

Table E.3
Cross-Tabulation of Support for Military Action in Afghanistan and Expected Casualties,
November 2001

Q2. Do you support or oppose the U.S. military action in Afghanistan?

Q7. How likely do you think it is that there will be a large number of U.S. military casualties in Afghanistan: very likely, somewhat likely, somewhat unlikely, or very unlikely?

	% Support	% Oppose	N
Very likely	86	14	105
Somewhat likely	90	7	283
Somewhat unlikely	95	4	244
Very unlikely	94	6	107
Don't know/refused	67	11	20
Total	91	7	759

SOURCE: ABC News/Washington Post, November 27, 2001.
NOTE: p < 0.001 in a Chi-square test of independence.

This survey does not ask questions about consumption of information. But in Tables E.4 and E.5 we present cross-tabulations of the support for military action in Afghanistan by party and ideology: Chi-square tests of independence suggest that there is significant association between these variables and support for the military action in Afghanistan.

Table E.4
Cross-Tabulation of Support for Military Action in Afghanistan by Party, November 2001

2. Do you support or oppose the U.S. military action in Afghanistan?

Generally speaking, do you consider yourself a Democrat, Republican, or Independent?

	% Support	% Oppose	N
Democrat	89	8	237
Republican	98	2	236
Independent	87	11	205
Other	83	4	55
Don't know/refused	80	13	26
Total	91	7	759

SOURCE: ABC News/Washington Post, November 27, 2001.
NOTE: p < 0.001 in a Chi-square test of independence.

Table E.5
Cross-Tabulation of Support for Military Action in Afghanistan by Political Views, November 2001

2. Do you support or oppose the U.S. military action in Afghanistan?

Would you say your views on most political matters are liberal, moderate or conservative?

	% Support	% Oppose	N
Liberal	87	13	147
Moderate	92	5	343
Conservative	95	5	225
Don't know/refused	75	18	44
Total	91	7	759

SOURCE: ABC News/Washington Post, November 27, 2001.
NOTE: p < 0.001 in a Chi-square test of independence.

Cross-Tabulation of Independent Variables and Party

Cross-tabulations of the beliefs about stakes, prospects, and casualties by party (Tables E.6 through E.8) suggest that partisanship was also important in these beliefs. At the same time, we can often see that these influences are just of degree. Members of the president's party were more likely to take the most extreme position, while members of other parties were more moderate in their position. For example, Republicans were more likely to say that the United States should take a leading role in the military action against terrorism in Afghanistan, while Democrats were more likely to say that the United States should take a large role but not the leading role (Table E.6).

Table E.6
Cross-Tabulation of Stakes of the Campaign by Party, November 2001

8. When it comes to (READ ITEM) do you think the United States should take the leading role, a large role but not the lead, a lesser role or no role at all?

d. Taking military action against terrorist groups that try to reestablish themselves in Afghanistan

Generally speaking, do you consider yourself a Democrat, Republican, or Independent?

	Leading role	Large role, but not the lead	Lesser role	No role at all	N
Democrat	49	40	7	3	237
Republican	65	27	6	2	236
Independent	48	34	12	5	205
Other	65	21	11	1	55
Don't know/refused	40	35	4	4	26
Total	54	33	8	3	759

SOURCE: ABC News/Washington Post, November 27, 2001.
NOTE: $p < 0.001$ in a Chi-square test of independence.

The same pattern of the responses holds in the case of beliefs about prospects. Results in Table E.7 suggest that Republicans were more likely to respond that the military action in Afghanistan was going very well, while Democrats were more likely to reply that it was going fairly well. And Table E.8 shows that beliefs about the number of U.S. casualties also was associated with party orientation.

Table E.7
Cross-Tabulation of the Prospects of the Military Action in Afghanistan by Party, November 2001

Q5. Do you think the U.S. military action in Afghanistan is going very well, fairly well, not too well, or not well at all?

Generally speaking, do you consider yourself a Democrat, Republican, or Independent?

	Very well	Fairly well	Not too well	Not well at all	N
Democrat	34	61	3	1	237
Republican	55	42	1	1	236
Independent	37	53	5	3	205
Other	36	49	2	6	55
Don't know/refused	49	22	11	0	26
Total	42	51	3	2	759

SOURCE: ABC News/Washington Post, November 27, 2001.
NOTE: $p < 0.001$ in a Chi-square test of independence.

Table E.8
Cross-Tabulation of the Expectation of Casualties in the Military Action in Afghanistan by Party, November 2001

Q7. How likely do you think it is that there will be a large number of U.S. military casualties in Afghanistan: very likely, somewhat likely, somewhat unlikely or very unlikely?

Generally speaking, do you consider yourself a Democrat, Republican, or Independent?

	Very likely	Somewhat likely	Somewhat unlikely	Very unlikely	N
Democrat	20	39	26	11	237
Republican	9	36	37	17	236
Independent	12	37	35	14	205
Other	8	37	30	17	55
Don't know/refused	23	31	18	16	26
Total	14	37	32	14	759

SOURCE: ABC News/Washington Post, November 27, 2001.
NOTE: p < 0.001 in a Chi-square test of independence.

Results of Statistical Modeling

Afghanistan was a somewhat special case because support for the campaign was consistently so high. At the same time, the questions often provided us with information about the strength of a respondent's support for the campaign.

Table E.9 describes the questions we used to estimate the model.

Table E.9
Wording of Questions in ABC News/Washington Post War Poll #2, November 27, 2001

Variable	Question Wording
Support	2. Do you support or oppose the U.S. military action in Afghanistan? Do you support/oppose this strongly or somewhat?
Security interests	8d. When it comes to (READ ITEM), do you think the United States should take the leading role, a large role but not the lead, a lesser role, or no role at all?
	d. Taking military action against terrorist groups that try to reestablish themselves in Afghanistan
Prospects	5. Do you think the U.S. military action in Afghanistan is going very well, fairly well, not too well, or not well at all?
Costs	7. How likely do you think it is that there will be a large number of U.S. military casualties in Afghanistan: very likely, somewhat likely, somewhat unlikely, or very unlikely?

The nature of the data suggested that we use ordered probit regression to identify the patterns in support, as this method would take into account all available information. Ordered probit regression makes several important assumptions about the data, which need to be confirmed before employing the technique. First, ordered probit regression assumes that the odds are proportional between categories; in other words, it assumes that coefficients in different categories are the same. This assumption was satisfied in our dataset, so we chose to use ordered probit estimates.

As described in Table E.10, the model correctly classified about 85 percent of the respondents in terms of whether they approved or disapproved of the military action in Afghanistan. Again, the variables that are hypothesized to be the key drivers of support and opposition contributed the most: the reduced-form model, which included only beliefs about the stakes, prospects for success, and costs, predicted support or opposition for fully 84 percent of the respondents, and when party and information were added, the model predicted 85 percent, a very slight improvement over the reduced-form model. We also estimated a number of other models using two other datasets that had differently worded questions; these correctly predicted approval or disapproval in 79–85 percent of the cases.

From these results we can see that all four of the key variables—perceived stakes (in this case, security interests), prospects for success, casualties, and party—were statistically significant, although their generally small size raises questions about their substantive significance. Put another way, because eight in ten or more had favorable beliefs and approved of the war, it seems there was not much variation left to account for.

Although it was not statistically significant, race was the most important predictor of support; this was followed by respondents' assessments of the prospects for success, party, perceptions of stakes, and, finally, expectations of casualties.

It should be noted that although the direction of the coefficients was as predicted in all cases, the specific values of the coefficients in the model presented here were affected by the nature (both structure and wording) of the specific questions asked; estimation of another model based on a survey conducted at the end of September, for example, suggested that the perceived stakes (and not the prospects for success) were the most important predictors of support and opposition; this model also suggested that the impact of casualties was negative but, in this case, not statistically significant.

Based on our analyses of three datasets for Afghanistan, we can, however, say that casualties were consistently the least important determinant of support or opposition to military action in Afghanistan, suggesting that most Americans were far more concerned about effectively eliminating the threat than minimizing U.S. casualties, a striking contrast to the results for Somalia, Haiti, Bosnia, and, to an extent, Kosovo.

Table E.10
Marginal Probability from the Probit Estimates of Approval (Q2)

Variables	Change in Probability at Mean Values	Change in Probability at Mean Values
Stakes (Q8d)	0.012 (0.007)*	0.012 (0.007)*
Prospects (Q5)	0.023 (0.007)***	0.024 (0.007)***
Casualties (Q7)	−0.009 (0.005)*	−0.009 (0.005)*
Party 1 if Democrat[†]	−0.003 (0.012)	−0.004 (0.013)
Party 1 if Independent[†]	−0.014 (0.012)	−0.015 (0.013)
Ideology 1 if liberal[†]		0.005 (0.009)
Ideology 1 if moderate[†]		0.003 (0.011)
Race 1 if black[†]	−0.051 (0.034)	−0.052 (0.034)
Gender 1 if female[†]	0.007 (0.008)	0.006(0.008)
Education 1 if less than high school[†]		−0.006 (0.013)
Education 1 if some college[†]		−0.005 (0.011)
Education 1 if college graduate[†]		−0.005 (0.013)
Education 1 if postgraduate[†]		−0.018 (0.022)
Wald Chi-square (Prod > Chi2)	54.76 (0.000)	60.28 (0.000)
Log-likelihood	−85.75	−85.00
Observations	711	711
% correctly specified	84%	85%

SOURCE: ABC News/Washington Post, November 27, 2001.
[†] dF/dx is for discrete change of dummy variable from 0 to 1.
* Significant at 10%.
** Significant at 5%
*** Significant at 1%.
Robust standard error in parentheses.

Statistical Results for Iraq

Support and Weapons of Mass Destruction

Because the issue of Iraqi weapons of mass destruction was so prominent before and after the war, it is worth presenting the results of our analyses of the relationship between support and beliefs about weapons of mass destruction over time.

Table F.1 cross-tabulates results from an October 2002 poll by the Pew Research Center on support for taking military action and beliefs about Iraqi nuclear weapons. As shown, about two-thirds of those who believed that Iraq was close to or already had nuclear weapons supported military action, whereas fewer than four in ten of those who did not believe this supported such action.

Table F.1

Cross-Tabulation of Support for Military Action in Iraq and Beliefs About Iraq's Ability to Develop Weapons of Mass Destruction, October 2002

Would you favor or oppose taking military action in Iraq to end Saddam Hussein's rule?

What's your opinion based on what you've heard or read: Is Saddam Hussein close to having nuclear weapons, or is he a long way from getting nuclear weapons?

	% Favor	% Oppose	N
Close to having nuclear weapons	67	26	604
Long way from getting	37	53	96
[Volunteered] Already has weapons	68	22	133
Don't know/refused	48	29	96
Total	62	28	928

SOURCE: Pew, October 2–6, 2002.
NOTE: $p < 0.001$ in a Chi-square test of independence.

At the same time we can see that beliefs about presence of the WMD in Iraq in October 2002 did not differ in a statistically significant fashion by party (Table F.2).[3]

---

[3]Our analyses showed that the probability of supporting military action was also higher among those who believed that Iraq assisted the 9/11 terrorists, and that that belief also had a partisan cast to it: Republicans were far more likely than Democrats to believe that Iraq had helped the terrorists.

Table F.2
Cross-Tabulation of the Belief in the Presence of WMD in Iraq by Party, October 2002

What's your opinion based on what you've heard or read: Is Saddam Hussein close to having nuclear weapons, or is he a long way from getting nuclear weapons?

In politics today, do you consider yourself a Republican, Democrat, or Independent?

	% Close to having nuclear weapons	% Long way from getting nuclear weapons	% Already has nuclear weapons	N
Republican	72	5	14	271
Independent	63	14	14	274
Democrat	63	12	13	302
No preference	59	7	21	47
Other	67	0	0	6
Don't know/refused	46	13	22	28
Total	65	10	14	928

SOURCE: Pew, October 2–6, 2002.
NOTE: $p < 0.1009$ in a Chi-square test of independence.

By March 2003, 64 percent of those who felt that the United States would only be able to justify the war if it found Iraqi WMD supported going to war, whereas 85 percent of those who felt the United States could justify the war for other reasons supported action (Table F.3). It also continued to be true that Republicans were far more likely than Democrats or Independents to believe that the war could be justified even if WMD was not found (Table F.4).

Table F.3
Cross-Tabulation of Support for War and Justification for War with Iraq, March 2003

As you may know, the United States went to war with Iraq last night. Do you support or oppose the United States having gone to war with Iraq?

Do you think the United States will be able to justify this war ONLY if it finds weapons of mass destruction, such as chemical or biological weapons, in Iraq; or do you think the United States will be able to justify this war for other reasons, even if it does NOT find weapons of mass destruction in Iraq?

	% Support	% Oppose	N
Justify only if it finds weapons	64	35	174
Justify for the other reasons	85	13	264
[Volunteered] Neither/no justification	23	77	35
Don't know/refused	62	21	34
Total	72	26	506

SOURCE: ABC News/Washington Post, March 20, 2003.
NOTE: $p < 0.001$ in a Chi-square test of independence.

Table F.4
Cross-Tabulation of Justification for War by Party, March 2003

15. Do you think the United States will be able to justify this war ONLY if it finds weapons of mass destruction, such as chemical or biological weapons, in Iraq; or do you think the United States will be able to justify this war for other reasons, even if it does NOT find weapons of mass destruction in Iraq?

Generally speaking, do you usually think of yourself as a Republican, Democrat, or Independent?

	% Justify only if it finds weapons	% Justify for the other reasons, even if it does not find weapons	[Volunteered] % Neither/ no justification	N
Republican	30	62	2	155
Independent	39	49	6	160
Democrat	37	45	9	149
Other	28	48	21	29
Don't know/refused	7	46	16	13
Total	34	52	7	506

SOURCE: ABC News/Washington Post, March 20, 2003.
NOTE: $p < 0.001$ in a Chi-square test of independence.

By April, more than eight in ten of those who thought the United States could justify the war for other reasons continued to support the war, while only slightly more than half of those who felt that finding WMD was necessary to justify the war supported (Table F.5). However, nearly seven in ten Independents and more than half of Democrats expressed the belief that the war could be justified for reasons other than WMD, more than in the March poll (Table F.6).

Table F.5
Cross-Tabulation of Support for War in Iraq and Justification for War, April 2003

Do you support or oppose the United States having gone to war with Iraq?

Do you think the United States will be able to justify this war ONLY if it finds weapons of mass destruction, such as chemical or biological weapons, in Iraq; or do you think the United States will be able to justify this war for other reasons, even if it does NOT find weapons of mass destruction in Iraq?

	% Support	% Oppose	N
Justify only if it finds weapons	53	43	110
Justify for other reasons	84	13	354
[Volunteered] Neither/no justification	38	53	34
Don't know/refused	60	24	14
Total	74	23	511

SOURCE: ABC News/Washington Post, April 3, 2003.
NOTE: $p < 0.001$ in a Chi-square test of independence.

Table F.6
Cross-Tabulation of Justification for War in Iraq by Party, April 2003

Do you think the United States will be able to justify this war ONLY if it finds weapons of mass destruction, such as chemical or biological weapons, in Iraq; or do you think the United States will be able to justify this war for other reasons, even if it does NOT find weapons of mass destruction in Iraq?

Generally speaking, do you usually think of yourself as a Republican, Democrat, or Independent?

	% Justify only if it finds weapons	% Justify for other reasons, even if it does NOT find weapons	[Volunteered] % Neither/ no justification	N
Republican	11	84	2	166
Independent	21	69	9	166
Democrat	32	56	7	140
Other	30	47	16	30
Don't know/refused	20	68	12	9
Total	21	69	7	511

SOURCE: ABC News/Washington Post, April 3, 2003.
NOTE: p < 0.001 in a Chi-square test of independence.

By June 2003, whereas more than three out of four (77 percent) Republicans and six in ten (62 percent) of Independents continued to say that they thought the war could be justified even if WMDs were not found, fewer than half (48 percent) of Democrats said so.[4] Put another way, finding Iraqi weapons of mass destruction increasingly became a *sine qua non* for support from some Democrats.

Iraq: Pre-War Opinions

In the case of Iraq we had four possible questionnaires that offered all the questions of interest: Gallup, January 3–5, 2003; ABC News/Washington Post, March 20, 2003 (ICPSR #3778); ABC News/Washington Post, March 23, 2003 (ICPSR#3779); and ABC News/ Washington Post, April 3, 2003 (ICPSR#3783).

Here we present the results from the two datasets that had the questions that were most relevant to our conceptual framework of stakes, prospects, costs, party, and information. One of the surveys was conducted before the war but at a time when there was significant discussion about the likelihood of war in the press (Gallup, January 3–5, 2003). The other survey (ABC News/Washington Post, March 20, 2003) was conducted just after the war started and can help to explain some of the covariates that were important at that time.

Our models did quite a good job in predicting approval. Using different combinations of questions from different surveys, the models correctly specified from 72 to 85 percent of cases, with all of the variables of interest assuming values in the predicted direction.

---

[4]ABC News/Washington Post poll, "Public Disquiet Grows With Casualties in Iraq," June 23, 2003.

Cross-Tabulations of Support and Independent Variables

Table F.7 presents a cross-tabulation of support for war in Iraq and beliefs about Iraq's military and weapon capabilities from the dataset for the Gallup poll that was conducted January 3–5, 2003. As shown, perceptions of security interests in the prospective war were significantly associated with support for going to war.

Table F.7
Cross-Tabulation of Support for War in Iraq and Interests, January 2003

Q9. All in all, do you think the current situation in Iraq is worth going to war over, or not?

Q10. Which of these statements do you think best describes Iraq's military and weapons capabilities?

	% Yes, worth going to war over	% No, not worth going to war over	N
It is a crisis for the United States	85	11	125
It is a major problem but is not a crisis	49	46	281
It is a minor problem	19	81	80
It is not a problem for the United States at all	56	44	18
Don't know/refused	35	35	9
Total	53	43	513

SOURCE. Gallup, January 3–5, 2003.
NOTE: p < .001 in a Chi-square test of independence.

A cross-tabulation of support for war in Iraq with judgments about the prospects for the campaign's success suggests that those who believed it likely that the United States would win the war were also more likely to support the military campaign in Iraq (Table F.8).

Table F.8
Cross-Tabulation of Support for War in Iraq and Prospects of the Campaign, January 2003

Q9. All in all, do you think the current situation in Iraq is worth going to war over, or not?

Q12. Ultimately, how likely is it that the United States and its allies would win that war against Iraq? Is it very likely, somewhat likely, not too likely, or not at all likely

	% Yes, worth going to war over	% No, not worth going to war over	N
Very likely	57	40	402
Somewhat likely	41	51	91
Not too likely	19	70	12
Not at all likely	0	100	4
Don't know/refused	61	0	5
Total	53	43	513

SOURCE: Gallup, January 3–5, 2003.
NOTE: p < .001 in a Chi-square test of independence.

Table F.9 presents a cross-tabulation of support for war in Iraq with expected casualties of the campaign. As predicted, there is significant association between expected casualties and support for the war.

Table F.9
Cross-Tabulation of Support for War in Iraq and Expected Casualties, January 2003

Q9. All in all, do you think the current situation in Iraq is worth going to war over, or not?

Q13. How many Americans do you think would be killed before the war was over?

	% Yes, worth going to war over	% No, not worth going to war over	N
Less than 1000	64	33	152
1,000 or more but less than 3,000	53	43	82
3,000 or more but less than 5,000	43	57	38
5,000 or more but less than 10,000	55	40	26
10,000 or more but less than 15,000	53	44	16
15,000 or more but less than 20,000	78	22	8
20,000 or more but less than 30,000	37	63	21
30,000 or more but less than 40,000	0	100	3
40,000 or more but less than 50,000	19	81	4
50,000 or more	35	60	36
Don't know/refused	51	40	127
Total	53	43	513

SOURCE: Gallup, January 3–5, 2003.
NOTE: $p < .05$ in a Chi-square test of independence.

This poll also asked questions about how closely people were following the news about the situation involving Iraq. Table F.10 presents a cross-tabulation of support for war by party and self-reported consumption of information. Results of the Chi-square tests of independence suggest that, as predicted, the level of support increases for Republicans as their level of information increases. Support is not highly dependent on the consumption of information in the case of Democrats or Independents, however, which may be because Democratic leaders were somewhat divided over the matter of going to war against Iraq.

Table F.10
Cross-Tabulation of Support for War in Iraq and Consumption of Information by Party
(in Percentage and Number of Observations)

Q9. All in all, do you think the current situation in Iraq is worth going to war over, or not?

Q7. How closely have you been following the news about the situation involving Iraq?

Republicans:	% Yes, worth going to war over	% No, not worth going to war over	N
Very closely	80	18	81
Somewhat closely	76	20	76
Not too closely	25	47	5
Not at all	0	57	2
Total	75	20	163

Democrats:	% Yes, worth going to war over	% No, not worth going to war over	N
Very closely	47	50	74
Somewhat closely	49	45	86
Not too closely	56	38	27
Not at all	17	59	5
Total	48	46	192

Independents:	% Yes, worth going to war over	% No, not worth going to war over	N
Very closely	32	67	63
Somewhat closely	40	54	79
Not too closely	29	71	12
Not at all	0	73	5
Total	35	61	159

SOURCE: Gallup, January 3–5, 2003.
NOTE: $p < 0.001$ (Republican), $p < 0.5250$ (Democrat), $p < 0.2068$ (Independent) in a Chi-square test of independence.

Some additional support for the role of partisan and ideological leadership can be found in Tables F.11 and F.12; both were associated with the belief that it was worth going to war.

Table F.11
Cross-Tabulation of Support for War in Iraq by Party, January 2003

Q9. All in all, do you think the current situation in Iraq is worth going to war over, or not?

In politics, as of today, do you consider yourself a Republican, Democrat, or Independent?

	% Yes, worth going to war over	% No, not worth going to war over	N
Republican	75	20	163
Independent	49	47	179
Democrat	35	61	159
Don't know/refused	45	43	12
Total	53	43	513

SOURCE: Gallup, January 3–5, 2003.
NOTE: p < .001 in a Chi-square test of independence.

Table F.12
Cross-Tabulation of Support for War in Iraq by Political Views, January 2003

Q9. All in all, do you think the current situation in Iraq is worth going to war over, or not?

How do you describe your political views?

	% Yes, worth going to war over	% No, not worth going to war over	N
Very conservative	78	18	32
Conservative	70	26	167
Moderate	45	50	178
Liberal	39	58	97
Very liberal	19	81	25
Don't know/refused	43	20	13
Total	53	43	513

SOURCE: Gallup, January 3–5, 2003.
NOTE: p < .001 in a Chi-square test of independence.

Cross-Tabulations of Independent Variables and Party

Beliefs about the war in Iraq were more dependent on the respondent's party than they were in Operation Enduring Freedom. Results in Table F.13 suggest that Republicans were more likely to support war in Iraq than Democrats or Independents. Table F.14 suggests that beliefs about Iraq's weapons capabilities were also partisan-coded.

Table F.13
Cross-Tabulation of Support for Military Campaign in Iraq by Party, January 2003

Q9. All in all, do you think the current situation in Iraq is worth going to war over, or not?

In politics, as of today, do you consider yourself a Republican, Democrat, or Independent?

	% Yes, worth going to war over	% No, not worth going to war over	N
Republican	75	20	163
Democrat	35	61	159
Independent	49	47	179
Don't know/refused	45	43	12
Total	53	43	513

SOURCE: Gallup, January 3–5, 2003.
NOTE: p < .001 in a Chi-square test of independence.

Table F.14
Cross-Tabulation of the Stakes of the War in Iraq by Party, January 2003

Q10. Which of these statements do you think best describes Iraq's military and weapons capabilities?

In politics, as of today, do you consider yourself a Republican, Democrat, or Independent?

	% It is a crisis for the United States	% It is a major problem but is not a crisis	% It is a minor problem	% It is not a problem for the United States at all	N
Republican	32	55	9	3	314
Democrat	25	52	17	4	374
Independent	18	60	18	3	309
Don't know/refused	0	100	0	0	3
Total	25	56	14	3	1,000

SOURCE: Gallup, January 3–5, 2003.
NOTE: p < 0.0343 in a Chi-square test of independence.

Table F.15 suggests that beliefs about a successful outcome were also associated with partisanship, and Table F.16 demonstrates a statistically significant relationship between party and beliefs about likely casualties.

Table F.15
Cross-Tabulation of the Prospects of the War in Iraq by Party, January 2003

Q12. Ultimately, how likely is it that the United States and its allies would win that war against Iraq? Is it very likely, somewhat likely, not too likely, or not at all likely

In politics, as of today, do you consider yourself a Republican, Democrat, or Independent?

	% Very likely	% Somewhat likely	% Not too likely	% Not at all likely	N
Republican	89	11	1	0	314
Democrat	71	22	5	2	374
Independent	75	18	6	1	309
Don't know/refused	79	21	0	0	3
Total	78	17	4	1	1,000

SOURCE: Gallup, January 3–5, 2003.
NOTE: $p < 0.001$ in a Chi-square test of independence.

Table F.16
Cross-Tabulation of the Expected Casualties in the War with Iraq by Party, January 2003

Q13. How many Americans do you think would be killed before the war was over?

In politics, as of today, do you consider yourself a Republican, Democrat, or Independent?

	% Very closely	% Somewhat closely	% Not too closely	% Not at all	N
Republican	36	16	10	8	314
Democrat	27	16	10	23	374
Independent	27	12	15	19	309
Don't know/refused	0	0	0	0	3
Total	30	15	12	17	1,000

SOURCE: Gallup, January 3–5, 2003.
NOTE: $p < 0.001$ in a Chi-square test of independence.

Results of Statistical Modeling

Table F.17 details the questions we used in our modeling. The results of the probit regression (Table F.18) suggest that most of the bivariate relations that we have described in the cross-tabulations also stand up in the multivariate analysis.

Table F.17
Wording of Question in Gallup/CNN/USA Today Poll, January 3–5 2003

Variable	Question Wording
Support	Q9. All in all, do you think the current situation in Iraq is worth going to war over, or not?
Security interests	Q10. Which of these statements do you think best describes Iraq's military and weapons capabilities? 1 It is a crisis for the United States, 2 It is a major problem but is not a crisis, 3 It is a minor problem, (or) 4 It is not a problem for the United States at all.
Prospects	Q12. Ultimately, how likely is it that the United States and its allies would win that war against Iraq? Is it very likely, somewhat likely, not too likely, or not at all likely?
Costs	Q13. How many Americans do you think would be killed before the war was over?
Info	Q7. How closely have you been following the news about the situation involving Iraq?

Table F.18
Marginal Probability from the Probit Estimates of Approval (Q9)

Variable	Change in Probability at Mean Values	Change in Probability at Mean Values
Stakes (Q10)	0.322 (0.055)***	0.312 (0.058)***
Prospects (Q12)	0.099 (0.068)	0.107 (0.068)
Casualties (Q13)	−0.028 (0.012)**	−0.028 (0.012)**
Information consumption (Q7)	−0.026 (0.050)	−0.005 (0.054)
Party 1 if Independent[†]	−0.351 (0.079)***	−0.322 (0.087)***
Party 1 if Democrat[†]	−0.165 (0.079)**	−0.169 (0.083)**
Ideology 1 if liberal[†]		−0.212 (0.099)**
Ideology 1 if moderate[†]		−0.110 (0.074)
Race 1 if black[†]	−0.010 (0.106)	−0.081 (0.111)
Gender 1 if female[†]	−0.143 (0.065)**	−0.144 (0.067)**
Education 1 if less than high school[†]		−0.134 (0.141)
Education 1 if some college[†]		−0.029 (0.087)
Education 1 if college graduate[†]		0.018 (0.100)
Education 1 if postgraduate[†]		−0.120 (0.094)
Income		−0.064 (0.028)**
Wald Chi-square (Prod > Chi2)	78.65 (0.000)	93.90 (0.000)
Log-likelihood	−194.28	−185.383
Observations	369	369
% correctly specified	76%	78%

SOURCE: Gallup, January 3–5, 2003.
[†] dF/dx is for discrete change of dummy variable from 0 to 1.
* Significant at 10%.
** Significant at 5%.
*** Significant at 1%.
Robust standard error in parentheses.

For example, perceptions of security interests were the most important factor in support for the war in Iraq: the belief that Iraq's weapons capabilities were a threat to the United States increased the probability of support by 0.32. This seems quite natural, taking into account that the war itself had not yet started and that most of the discussion at the time was about the WMD in Iraq and how much time to give UN inspectors. The perceived prospects for success of the campaign were also highly correlated with the support for the war; the belief that the war had good prospects increased the probability of supporting by about 0.10. Those people who thought that the United States and its allies could win the war were also more likely to support the campaign. At the same time, increase in the expected casualties is associated with decreased support for the campaign.

In all, both the full and reduced-form model correctly predicted support or opposition for 76–78 percent of the respondents, and again, their predictive ability was primarily based upon beliefs about the stakes, prospects, and costs of a conflict in Iraq.

Iraq: Modeling Public Opinion During the War

The second dataset is from surveys conducted after the war against Iraq started.

Cross-Tabulations of Support and Independent Variables

Results of our cross-tabulations and tests of independence suggest that the bivariate correlation patterns also hold in this case. For example, Table F.19 suggests that there is significant association between support for war in Iraq and beliefs about vital interests (note also that nearly three in four believed that the United States had vital interests at stake in Iraq).

Table F.19
Cross-Tabulation of Support for War in Iraq and Vital Interests, March 2003

3. As you may know, the United States went to war with Iraq last night. Do you support or oppose the United States having gone to war with Iraq?

11. Do you think America's vital interests are at stake in the situation involving Iraq, or not?

	% Support	% Oppose	N
Yes	82	16	334
No	48	52	130
Don't know/refused	70	23	42
Total	72	26	506

SOURCE: ABC News/Washington Post, March 20, 2003.
NOTE: $p < 0.001$ in a Chi-square test of independence.

Table F.20 shows that support for war in Iraq was systematically associated with the perceived prospects for success, as judged by the expected length of the military involvement.

Table F.20
Cross-Tabulation of Support for War in Iraq and Prospects of the Campaign, March 2003

3. As you may know, the United States went to war with Iraq last night. Do you support or oppose the United States having gone to war with Iraq?

13. Just your best guess, how long do you think the war with Iraq will last: days, weeks, months, about a year, or longer than that?

	% Support	% Oppose	N
Days	68	32	40
Weeks	78	19	152
Months	73	25	187
About a year	73	23	43
Longer than that	49	49	53
Don't know/refused	81	13	31
Total	72	26	506

SOURCE: ABC News/Washington Post, March 20, 2003.
NOTE: $p < 0.0030$ in a Chi-square test of independence.

Table F.21 presents evidence that support for the war was associated with expectations about the level of casualties that would be suffered by the U.S. military: again, those who expected significant U.S. casualties were less likely to support the war.

Table F.21
Cross-Tabulation of Support for War in Iraq and Expected Casualties, March 2003

3. As you may know, the United States went to war with Iraq last night. Do you support or oppose the United States having gone to war with Iraq?

14. Do you think there will or will not be a significant number of U.S. military casualties in the war with Iraq?

	% Support	% Oppose	N
Yes, there will	62	37	189
No, there will not	81	17	274
Don't know/refused	64	29	44
Total	72	26	506

SOURCE: ABC News/Washington Post, March 20, 2003.
NOTE: $p < 0.001$ in a Chi-square test of independence.

This survey did not ask anything about consumption of information, so we present a cross-tabulation of support for war by party; as shown, support for war was closely associated with partisanship as well (Table F.22): members of the president's party were more likely to support the United States going to war with Iraq.

Table F.22
Cross-Tabulation of Support for War in Iraq by Party, March 2003

3. As you may know, the United States went to war with Iraq last night. Do you support or oppose the United States having gone to war with Iraq?

Generally speaking, do you usually think of yourself as a Republican, Democrat, or Independent?

	% Support	% Oppose	N
Republican	90	8	155
Independent	73	24	160
Democrat	51	47	149
Other	76	20	29
Don't know/refused	77	23	13
Total	72	26	506

SOURCE: ABC News/Washington Post, March 20, 2003.
NOTE: $p < 0.001$ in a Chi-square test of independence.

Cross-Tabulation of Independent Variables and Party

Table F.23 shows that beliefs that the United States had vital interests at stake in the situation with Iraq were associated with party: members of the president's party were more likely to think that important interests were at stake in the situation involving Iraq. Table F.24 shows that beliefs about the length of the war failed the Chi-square test of association.

Table F.23
Cross-Tabulation of the Beliefs About Vital Interests in Iraq by Party, March 2003

11. Do you think America's vital interests are at stake in the situation involving Iraq, or not?

Generally speaking, do you usually think of yourself as a Republican, Democrat, or Independent?

	% Yes	% No	N
Democrat	56	36	149
Republican	77	16	155
Independent	69	24	160
Other	52	39	29
Don't know/refused	54	8	13
Total	66	26	506

SOURCE: ABC News/Washington Post, March 20, 2003.
NOTE: $p < 0.001$ in a Chi-square test of independence.

Table F.24
Cross-Tabulation of the Expected Length of the War with Iraq by Party, March 2003

13. Just your best guess, how long do you think the war with Iraq will last: days, weeks, months, about a year, or longer than that?

Generally speaking, do you usually think of yourself as a Republican, Democrat, or Independent?

	% Days	% Weeks	% Months	% About a Year	% Longer than that	N
Democrat	7	32	36	8	12	149
Republican	8	33	41	6	6	155
Independent	7	28	37	11	13	160
Other	10	20	31	17	14	29
Don't know/refused	7	23	15	7	16	13
Total	8	30	37	9	10	506

SOURCE: ABC News/Washington Post, March 20, 2003.
NOTE: $p < 0.1060$ in a Chi-square test of independence.

Table F.25 shows that expectations regarding casualties were associated with party: namely, Republicans had much smaller expectations about U.S. military casualties in the war with Iraq than Democrats.

Table F.25
Cross-Tabulation of the Expected Casualties in the War with Iraq by Party, March 2003

14. Do you think there will or will not be a significant number of U.S. military casualties in the war with Iraq?

Generally speaking, do you usually think of yourself as a Republican, Democrat, or Independent?

	% Yes, there will	% No, there will not	N
Democrat	42	52	149
Republican	30	63	155
Independent	40	48	160
Other	38	62	29
Don't know/refused	38	31	13
Total	37	54	506

SOURCE: ABC News/Washington Post, March 20, 2003.
NOTE: $p < 0.0034$ in a Chi-square test of independence.

Results of Statistical Modeling

Although the bivariate associations generally were as we would have expected, we are more interested in how the variables perform in the multivariate analysis. Table F.26 summarizes the variable we used in our logistic regression modeling, and Table F.27 presents the results from the logistic regression.

Table F.26
Wording of Question in ABC/WP War Poll #1, Marsh 2003

Variable	Wording of Question
Support	3. As you may know, the United States went to war with Iraq last night. Do you support or oppose the United States having gone to war with Iraq?
Benefits	11. Do you think America's vital interests are at stake in the situation involving Iraq, or not?
Prospects	13. Just your best guess, how long do you think the war with Iraq will last: days, weeks, months, about a year, or longer than that?
Costs	14. Do you think there will or will not be a significant number of U.S. military casualties in the war with Iraq?

As shown in Table F.27, the model correctly specified about 75 percent of the cases in the dataset. Vital interests influenced support for the war the most (in most other cases we examined, the coefficient on this variable was not so large); put another way, support was most closely associated with the various reasons that Americans had for believing that the United States had vital interests in Iraq. Those believing that there would be a significant number of casualties in the campaign were less likely to support the war, and a higher expected duration of the campaign was negatively related to support for the war, but not significantly so (the variable is coded such that the shorter the expected campaign, the better are the prospects).

Table F.27
Marginal Probability from the Probit Estimates of Approval (Q3)

Variables	Change in Probability at Mean Values
Vital interests (q11)	0.314 (0.054)***
Prospects (q13)	0.033 (0.021)
Casualties (q14)	−0.135 (0.050)***
Party 1 if Independent	−0.381 (0.065)***
Party 1 if Democrat	−0.159 (0.063)**
Female	−0.097 (0.045)**
Wald Chi-square (Prod > Chi2)	92.58
Log likelihood	−178.89
Observations	407
Correctly specified	75%

† dF/dx is for discrete change of dummy variable from 0 to 1.
* Significant at 10%.
** Significant at 5%.
*** Significant at 1%.
Robust standard error in parentheses.
SOURCE: ABC News/Washington Post March 20, 2003, N = 506.

The variables for perceived stakes, prospects for success, and costs were most responsible for the accuracy of the prediction: the reduced-form model correctly predicted support or opposition for 74.54 percent of the respondents.

To test the robustness of the model, we were also able to use the results of this model to predict responses in the other datasets. Although the questions about benefits were somewhat different in the other datasets, using the coefficients from Table F.27 we were able to correctly specify 83 percent of the *responses* in the ABC News/Washington Post March 23, 2003 poll, and 77 percent of the responses in the ABC News/Washington Post April 3, 2003 poll. This suggested that the model for Iraq was very robust.

Bibliography

ABC News. ABC News "Nightline" Somalia Poll, October 5, 1993 [Computer File]. ICPSR version. Radnor, PA: Chilton Research Services [producer], 1993. Ann Arbor, MI: Interuniversity Consortium for Political and Social Research [distributor], 1997.

ABC News. ABC News "Nightline" Haiti Poll, October 12, 1993 [Computer file]. ICPSR version. Radnor, PA: Chilton Research Services [producer], 1993. Ann Arbor, MI: Interuniversity Consortium for Political and Social Research [distributor], 1997.

ABC News/The Washington Post. ABC NEWS/WASHINGTON POST TERRORIST ATTACK POLL #3, SEPTEMBER 2001 [Computer file]. ICPSR version. Horsham, PA: Taylor Nelson Sofres Intersearch [producer], 2001. Ann Arbor, MI: Inter-university Consortium for Political and Social Research [distributor], 2001.

ABC News/The Washington Post. ABC NEWS/WASHINGTON POST WAR POLL #2, NOVEMBER 2001 [Computer file]. ICPSR version. Horsham, PA: Taylor Nelson Sofres Intersearch [producer], 2001. Ann Arbor, MI: Inter-university Consortium for Political and Social Research [distributor], 2002.

ABC News/The Washington Post. ABC NEWS/WASHINGTON POST WAR POLL #1, MARCH 2003 [Computer file]. ICPSR version. Horsham, PA: Taylor Nelson Sofres Intersearch [producer], 2003. Ann Arbor, MI: Inter-university Consortium for Political and Social Research [distributor], 2003.

ABC News/The Washington Post. ABC NEWS/WASHINGTON POST WAR POLL #2, MARCH 2003 [Computer file]. ICPSR version. Horsham, PA: Taylor Nelson Sofres Intersearch [producer], 2003. Ann Arbor, MI: Inter-university Consortium for Political and Social Research [distributor], 2003.

ABC News/The Washington Post. ABC NEWS/WASHINGTON POST WAR POLL #3, MARCH 2003 [Computer file]. ICPSR version. Horsham, PA: Taylor Nelson Sofres Intersearch [producer], 2003. Ann Arbor, MI: Inter-university Consortium for Political and Social Research [distributor], 2003.

ABC News/The Washington Post. ABC NEWS/WASHINGTON POST WAR POLL #1, APRIL 2003 [Computer file]. ICPSR version. Horsham, PA: Taylor Nelson Sofres Intersearch [producer], 2003. Ann Arbor, MI: Inter-university Consortium for Political and Social Research [distributor], 2003.

CBS News. CBS NEWS MONTHLY POLL #1, OCTOBER 2001 [Computer file]. ICPSR version. New York, NY: CBS News [producer], 2001. Ann Arbor, MI: Inter-university Consortium for Political and Social Research [distributor], 2002.

CBS News. CBS NEWS MONTHLY POLL #2, MARCH 1999 [Computer file]. ICPSR version. New York, NY: CBS News [producer], 1999. Ann Arbor, MI: Inter-university Consortium for Political and Social Research [distributor], 1999.

Gallup. Gallup/CNN/USA Today Poll: Haiti/Honesty and Ethical Standards, September 23–25, 1994 [Computer File]. Roper version. The Gallup Organization [producer], 1994. Storrs, CT: The Roper Center for Public Opinion Research [distributor], 1994.

Gallup. Gallup/CNN/USA Today Poll: Haiti/Honest and Ethical Standards, 23–25 September 1994 [Computer file]. Roper version. The Gallup Organization [producer], 1994. Roper Center for Public Opinion Research [distributor], 1994.

Gallup. Gallup/CNN/USA Today Poll: Bosnia Speech, November 27, 1995 [Computer File]. Roper version. The Gallup Organization [producer], 1995. Storrs, CT: The Roper Center for Public Opinion Research [distributor], 1995.

Gallup. Gallup/CNN/USA Today Poll: Congress/War on Terrorism/North Korea/2004 Presidential Election/Economy/Title Nine, January 3–5, 2003 [Computer File]. Roper version. The Gallup Organization [producer], 2003. Storrs, CT: The Roper Center for Public Opinion Research [distributor], 2003.

Pew Research Center. Kosovo News Interest Index, April 15–18, 1999 [Computer File]. Washington, D.C.: The Pew Research Center for the People and the Press [producer and distributor], 1999.

Pew Research Center. May News Interest Index, May 12–16, 1999 [Computer File]. Washington, D.C.: The Pew Research Center for the People and the Press [producer and distributor], 1999.

Pew Research Center. Early October 2002 Election Study, October 2–10, 2002 [Computer File]. Washington, D.C.: The Pew Research Center for the People and the Press [producer and distributor], 2003.